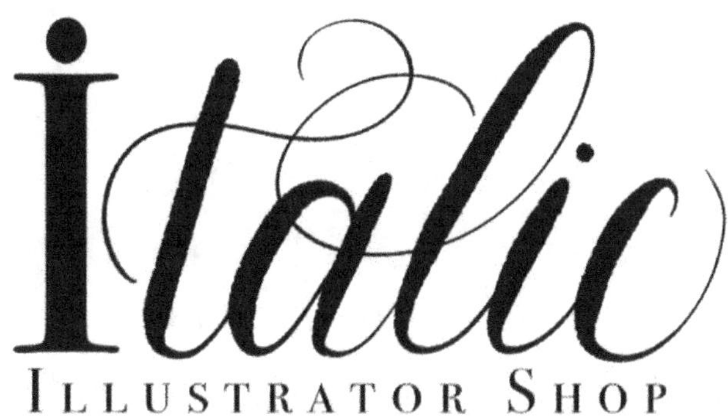

Italic
ILLUSTRATOR SHOP

WORKBOOK FOR BEGINNERS

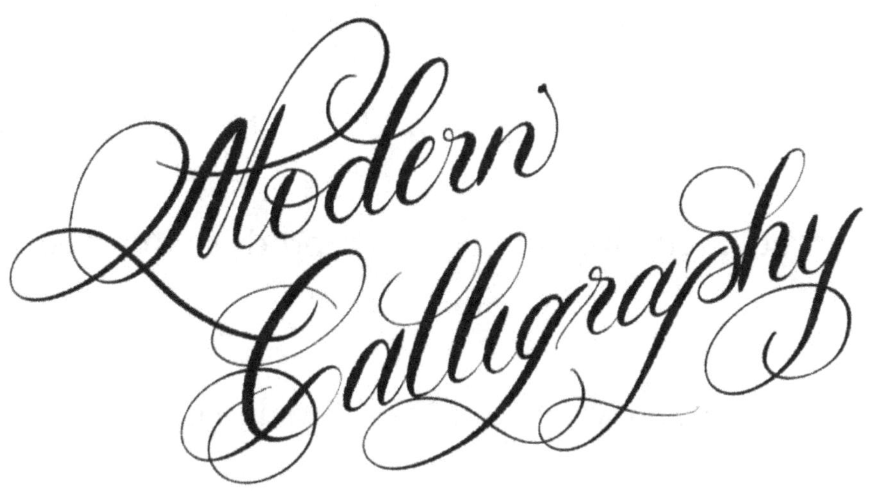

Modern Calligraphy

BY LYNNE LILLGE

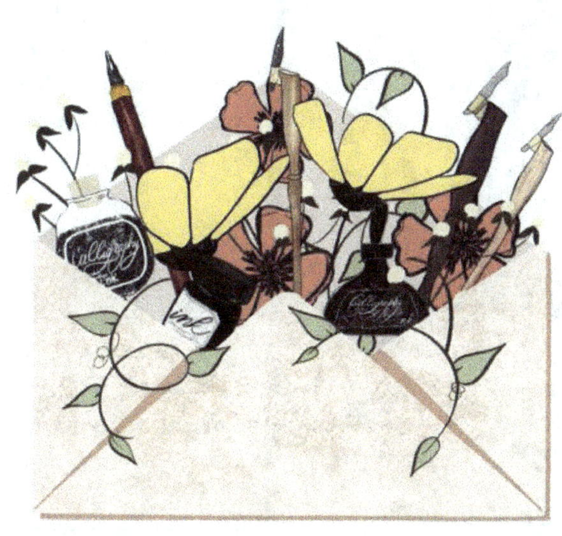

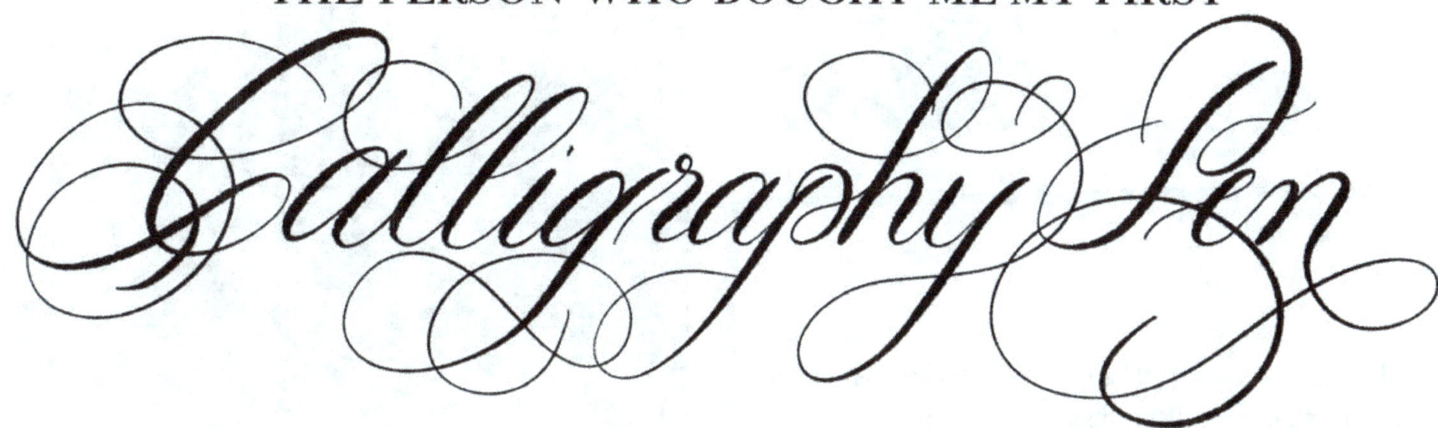
Calligraphy Pen

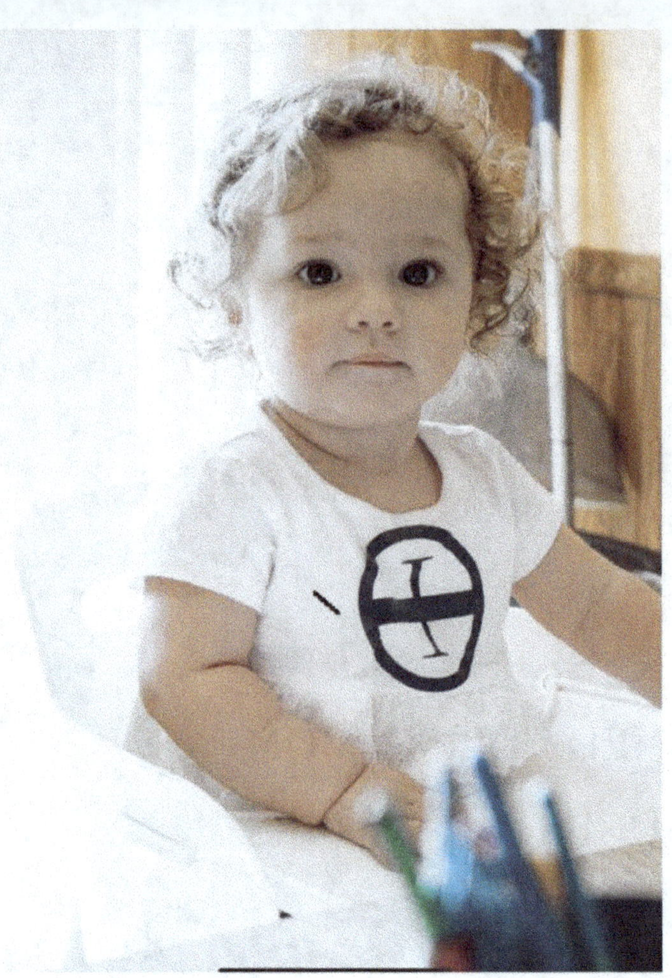

It all began when I relinquished my title as Director of Business Development at an advertising firm and chose to embody my life as an Artist living with her four magical lady cats.

Fast forward to today - the suits have been tucked away, replaced by paint covered tank tops full of saw dust and cat hair.

The cats are my coworkers-
my husband is my biggest fan-
Aleya and Easton my constant supervisors .

Yes—- I'm truly living my dreams.

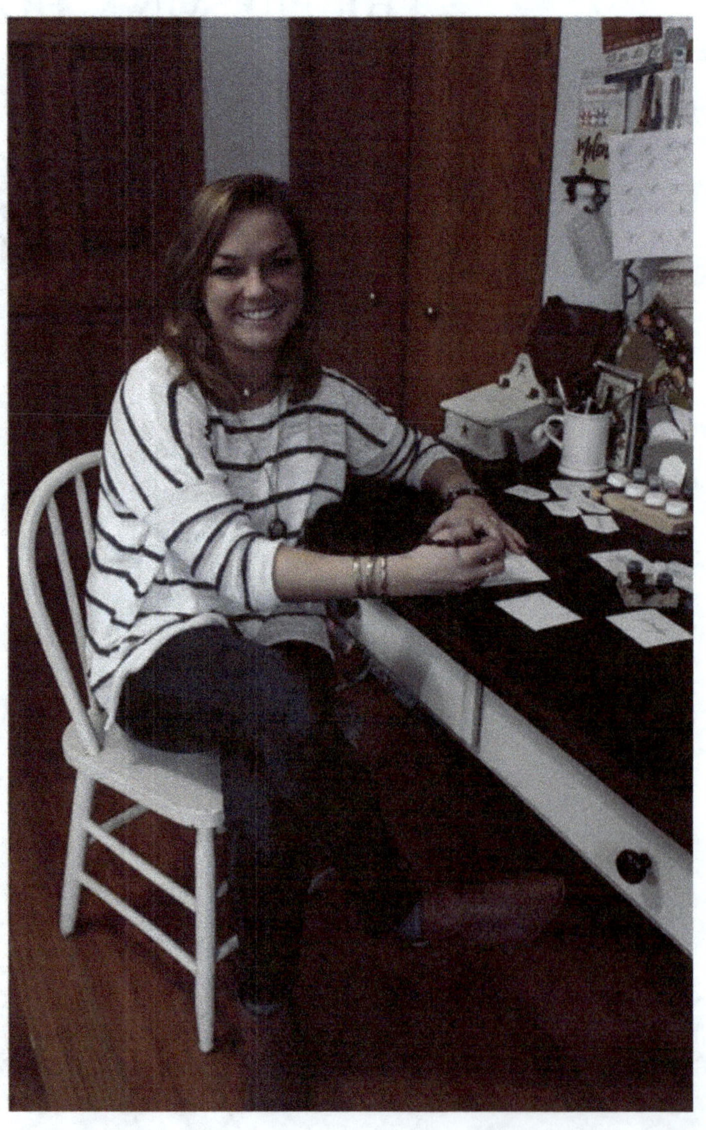

This book is meant for first time Calligraphers. If you have taken my class (or any beginners' course) then this is the workbook for you. The way to flourish in Calligraphy is to practice often. The goal is to create new muscle memory for how you write the alphabet. Practicing should be fun— not a chore. It is my hopes that this workbook will help you explore your calligraphy style and guide you to finding your own Modern Calligraphy Font.

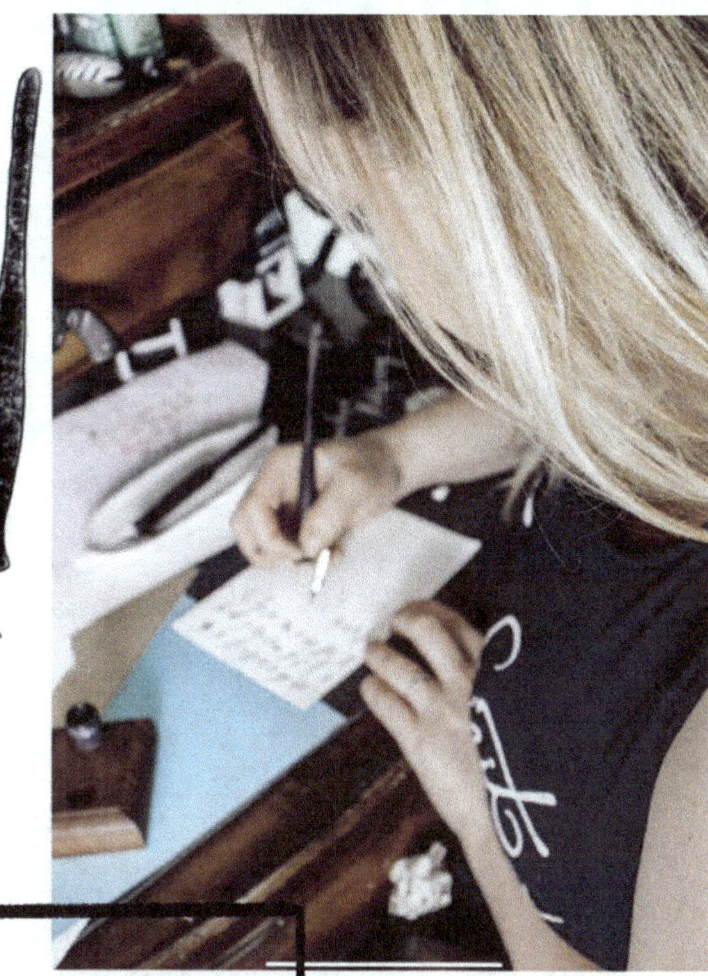

How to use
This Workbook

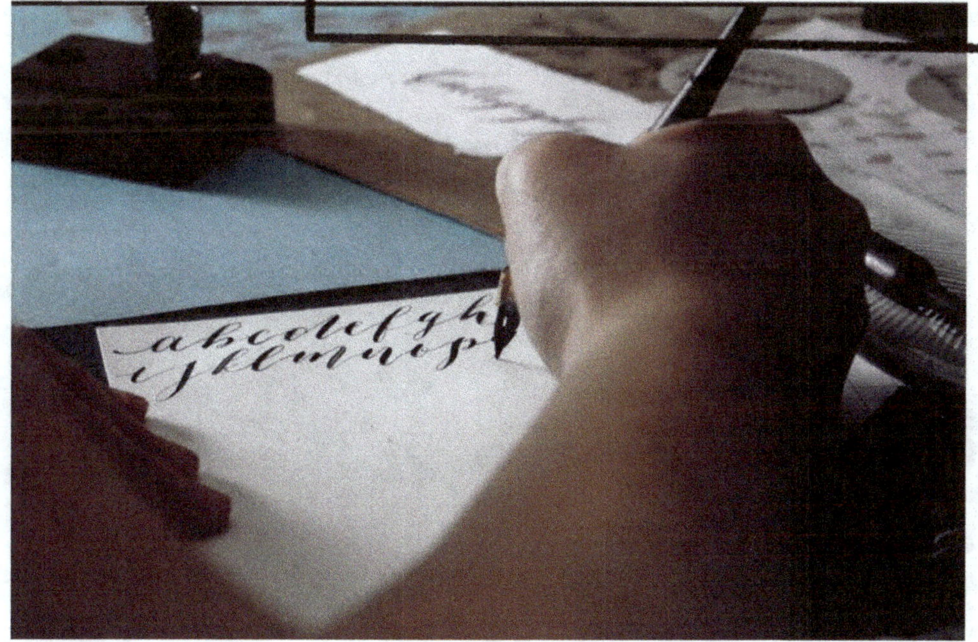

Written & Designed by Chelsey Lillge
Italic illustrator

-Waxseal Designer
-one of a kind wax seal handles
- Vintage postage Stamps
-unique Stationery
- Custom Calligraphy services

www.italicillustratorshop.com
Italic.illustrator@gmail.com

Calligraphy Pen

Nib holder- straight or oblique.
Most calligraphers recommend starting with an oblique because it helps the writer achieve the correct angles.

Paper

Heavy weight printer paper.
Card stock- not textured.
An ultra white, smooth uncoated paper is ideal for beginners.
Note: Calligraphy ink and paper should be paired together like dance partners. Some may look like they go together, yet they are just not in sync.
Inks can be too watery to suit the paper and will bleed into the wrong weighted paper.

Nibs

Nikko G Nibs are best for beginners. Be sure to clean new nibs with Dish soap or toothpaste to remove protective wax.

Ink

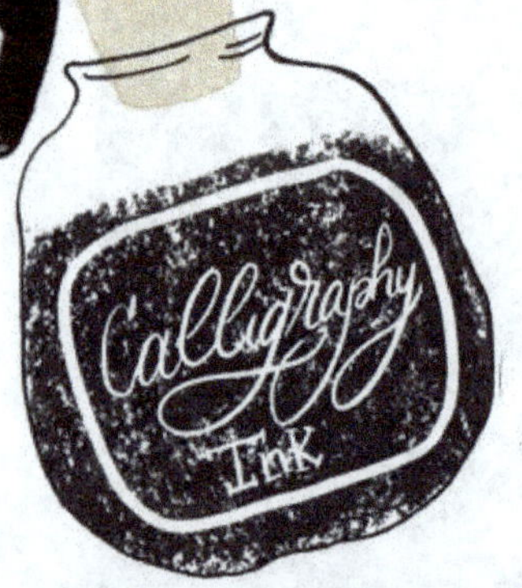

Sumi ink or Dr.PhMartin are my personal favorite for ink brands. Keep in mind, just like picking what pen best fits your hand, ink choice is the artist's preference.

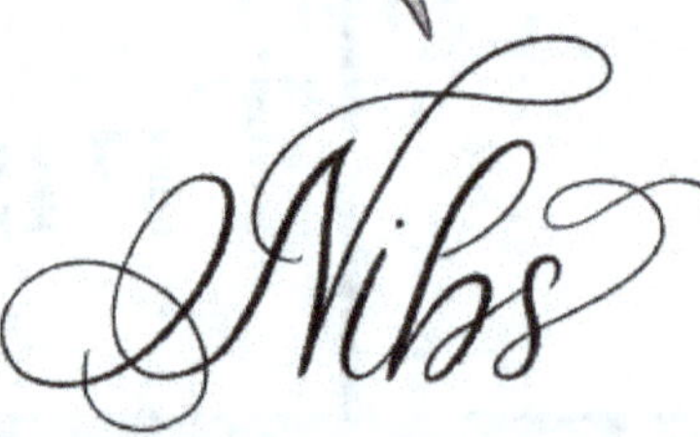

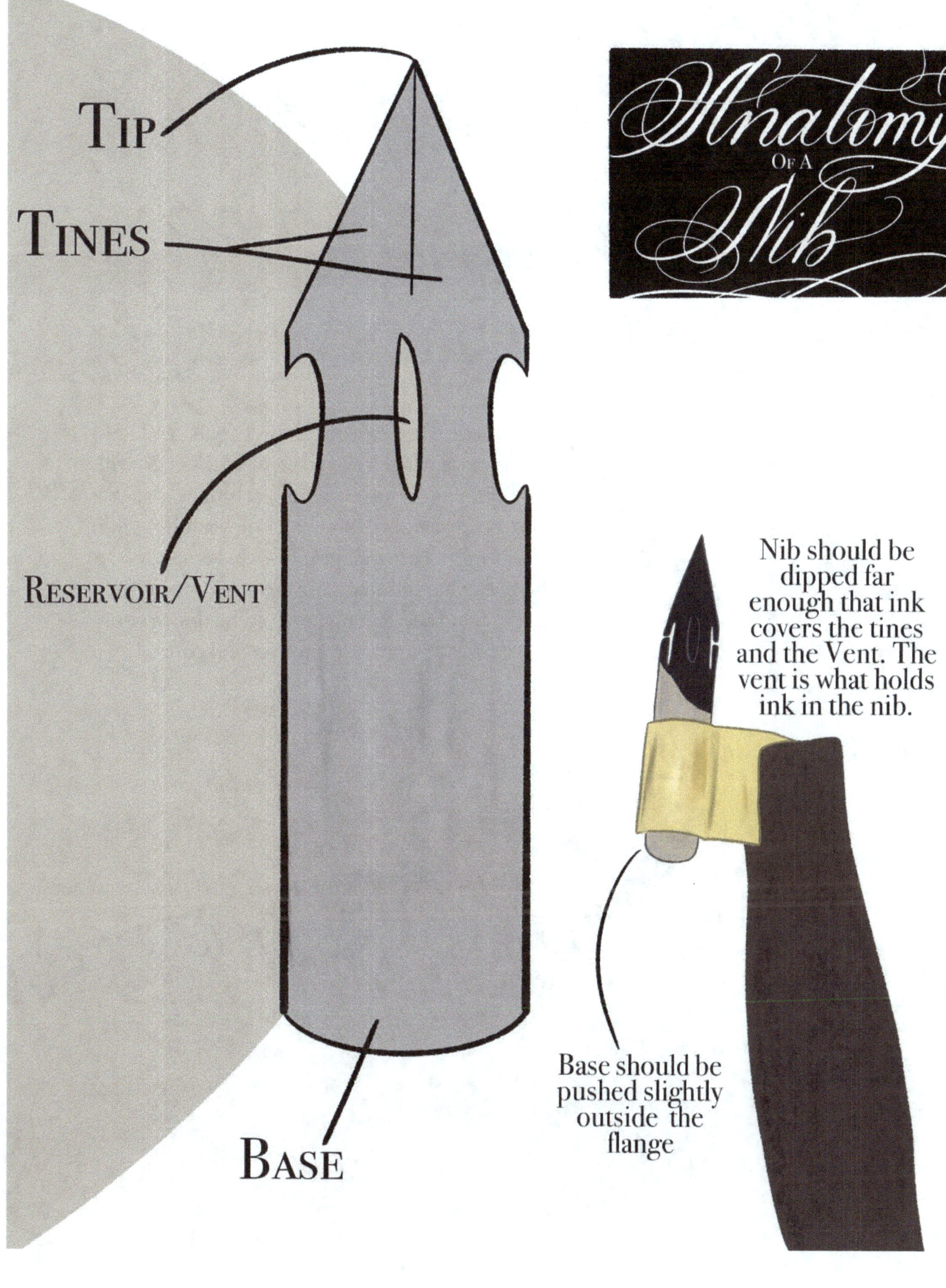

Anatomy
OF A
Nib

Tip

Tines

Reservoir/Vent

Base

Nib should be dipped far enough that ink covers the tines and the Vent. The vent is what holds ink in the nib.

Base should be pushed slightly outside the flange

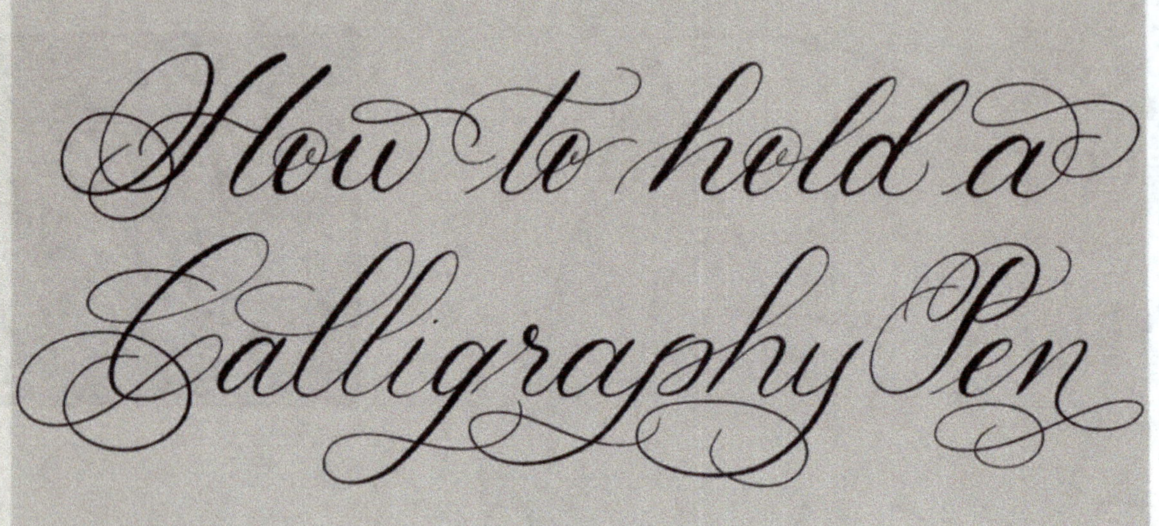

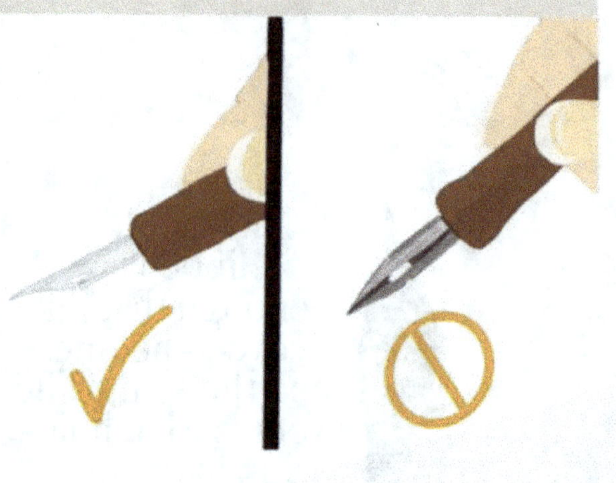

Sit on the edge of your chair, exhale, and hold your pen with a relaxed grip. Tight grips will hinder your flourishes and eventually give you writers' cramp. Remember, you want light fluid motions in your calligraphy— this is suppose to be a relaxing hobby. Your wrist should be flat on the table and feet planted on the floor. Your wrist will provide support and control.

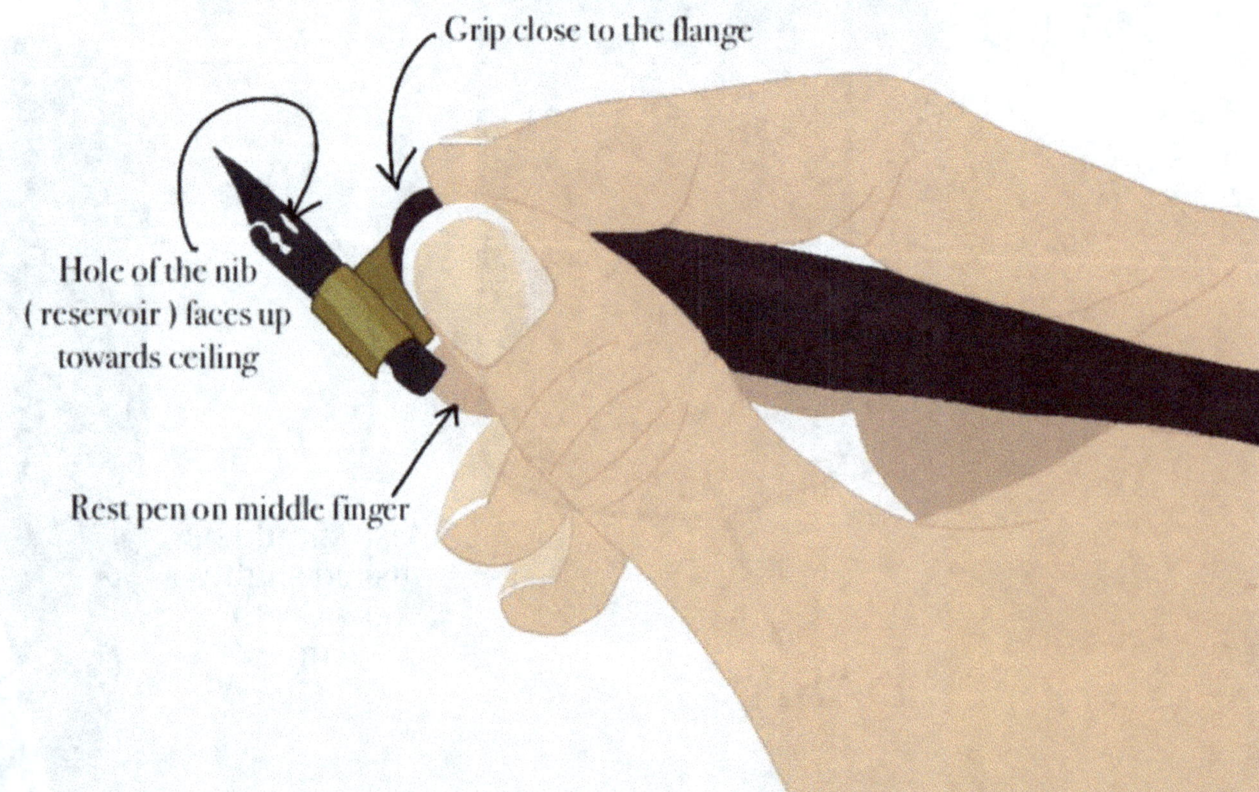

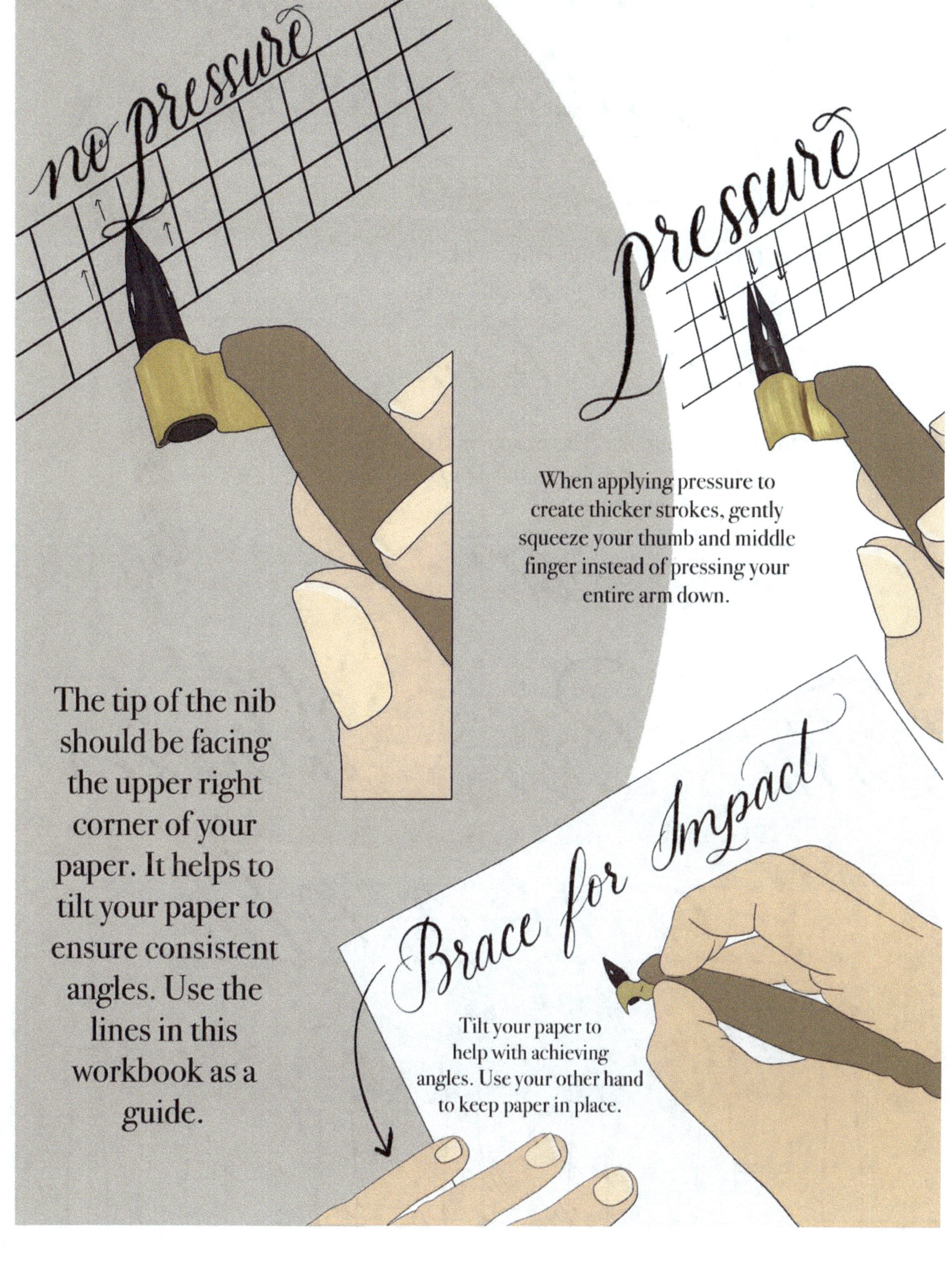

no pressure
Pressure
When applying pressure to create thicker strokes, gently squeeze your thumb and middle finger instead of pressing your entire arm down.
The tip of the nib should be facing the upper right corner of your paper. It helps to tilt your paper to ensure consistent angles. Use the lines in this workbook as a guide.
Brace for Impact
Tilt your paper to help with achieving angles. Use your other hand to keep paper in place.

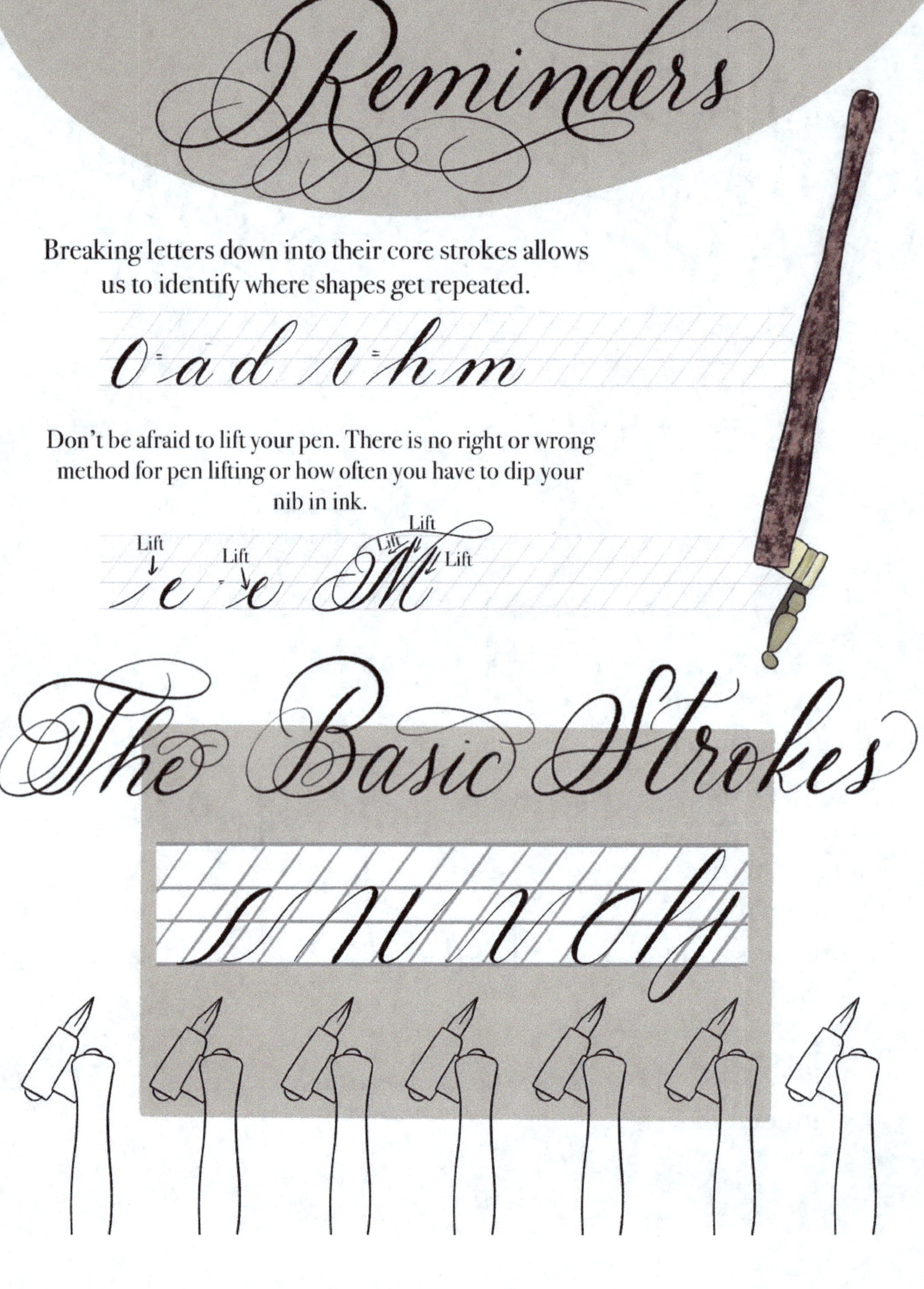

Reminders

Breaking letters down into their core strokes allows us to identify where shapes get repeated.

Don't be afraid to lift your pen. There is no right or wrong method for pen lifting or how often you have to dip your nib in ink.

The Basic Strokes

The Square Method

PRESSURE PRACTICE

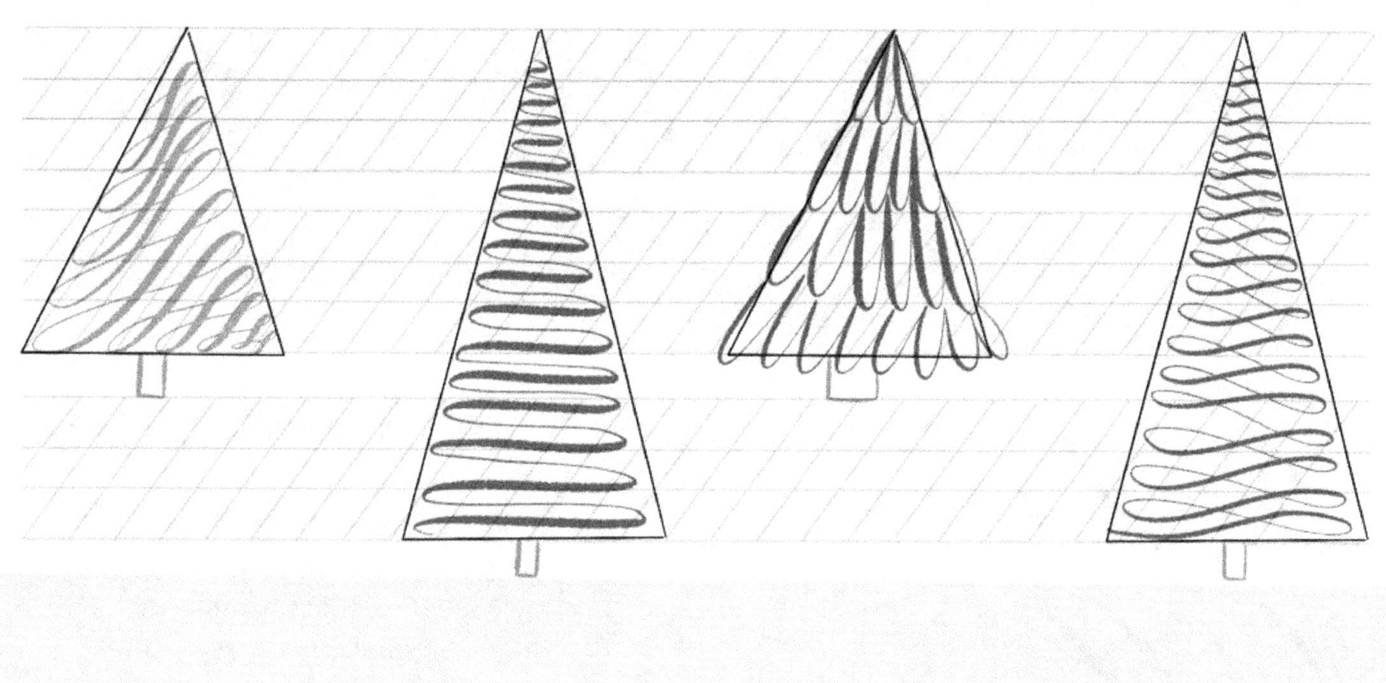

Connecting Letters

CONNECTORS

When forming words, focus on the connectors (the strokes that string each letter together. Connectors should be similar is size, style and distance .

CONSISTENTLY

Consistency of letter's strokes and angle are key for the 'Look' of your words. Pick a style and stick with it. Try writing out your word first and examine how it connects naturally. This will give you a template to guide your flourishes

CORRECT

INCORRECT

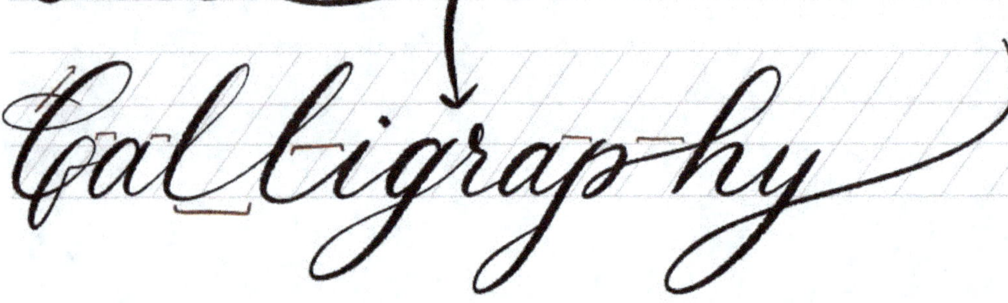

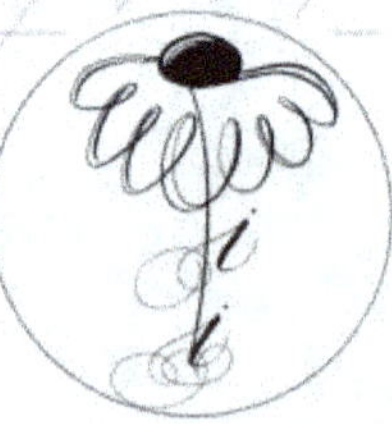

Style

bounce

stretch

classic

Flourish

hello

hello

hello

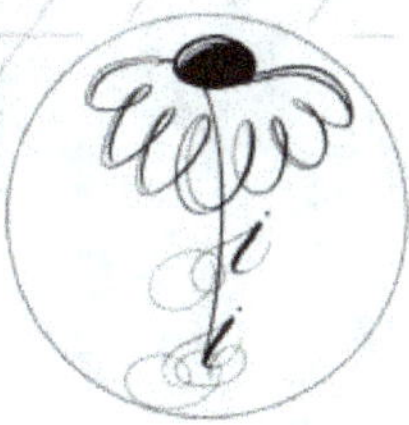

As an artist, you will add nuances to the letters, adapting and customizing alphabets to your style. If you are struggling with a word or letter write it in pencil and use it as a guide

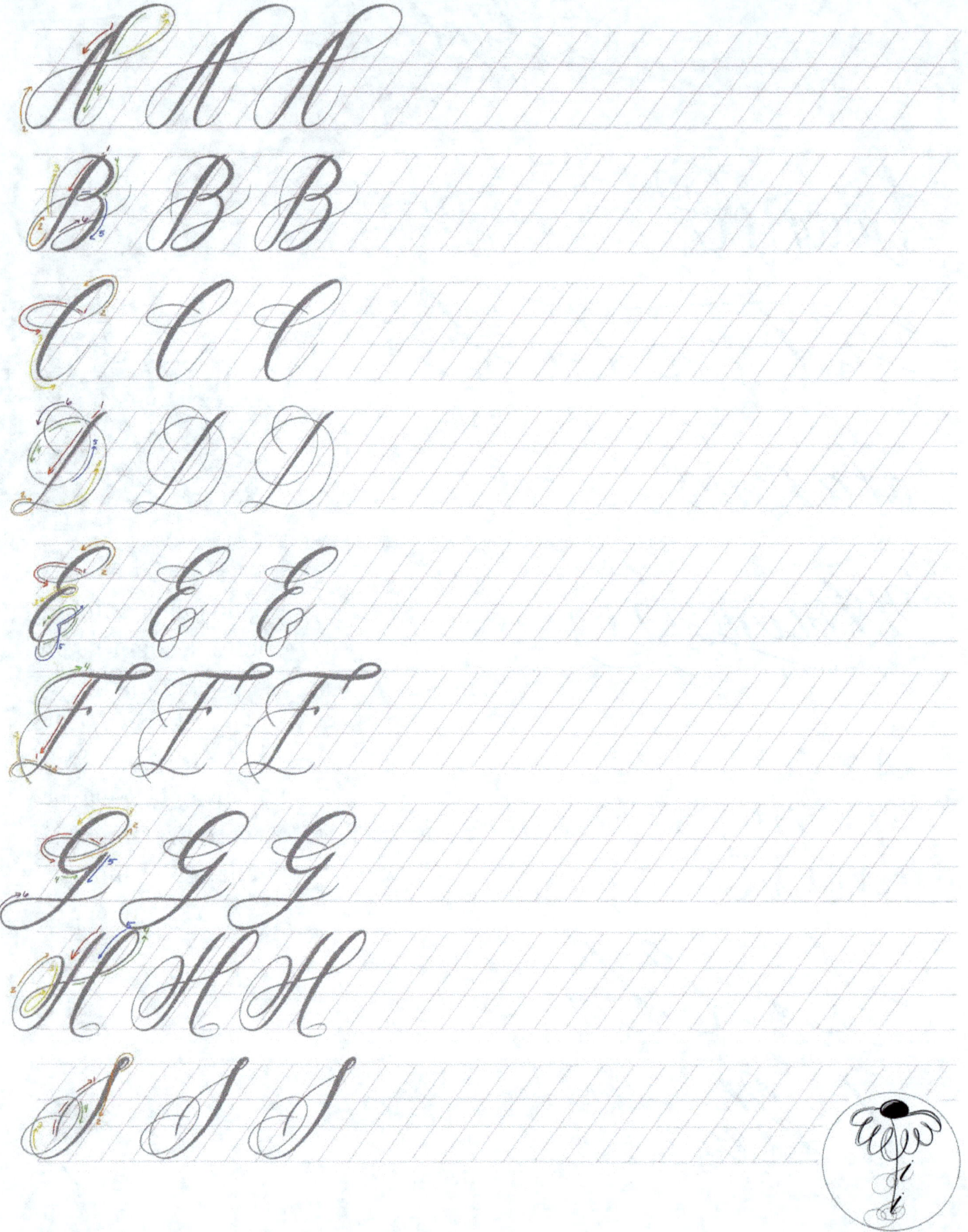

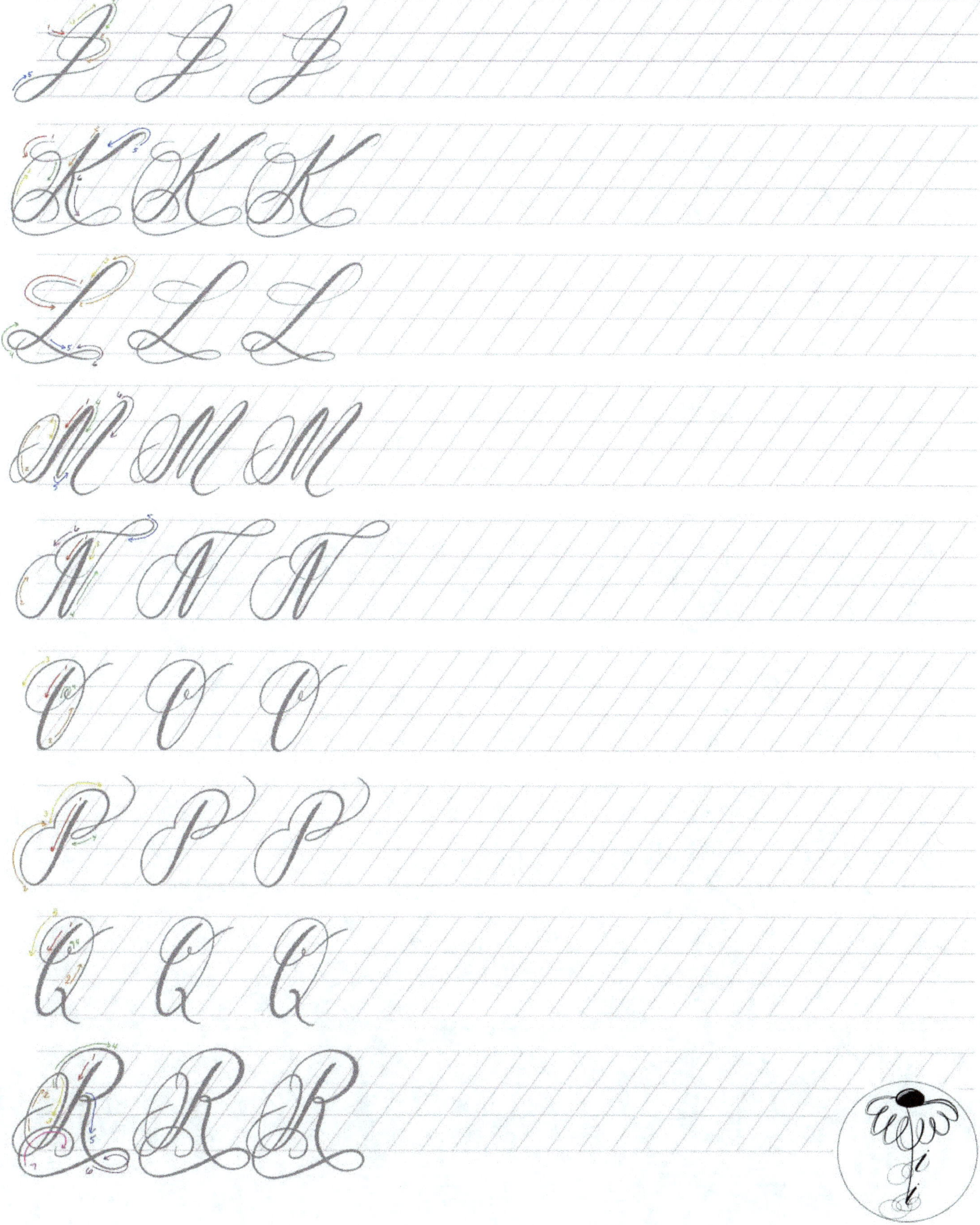

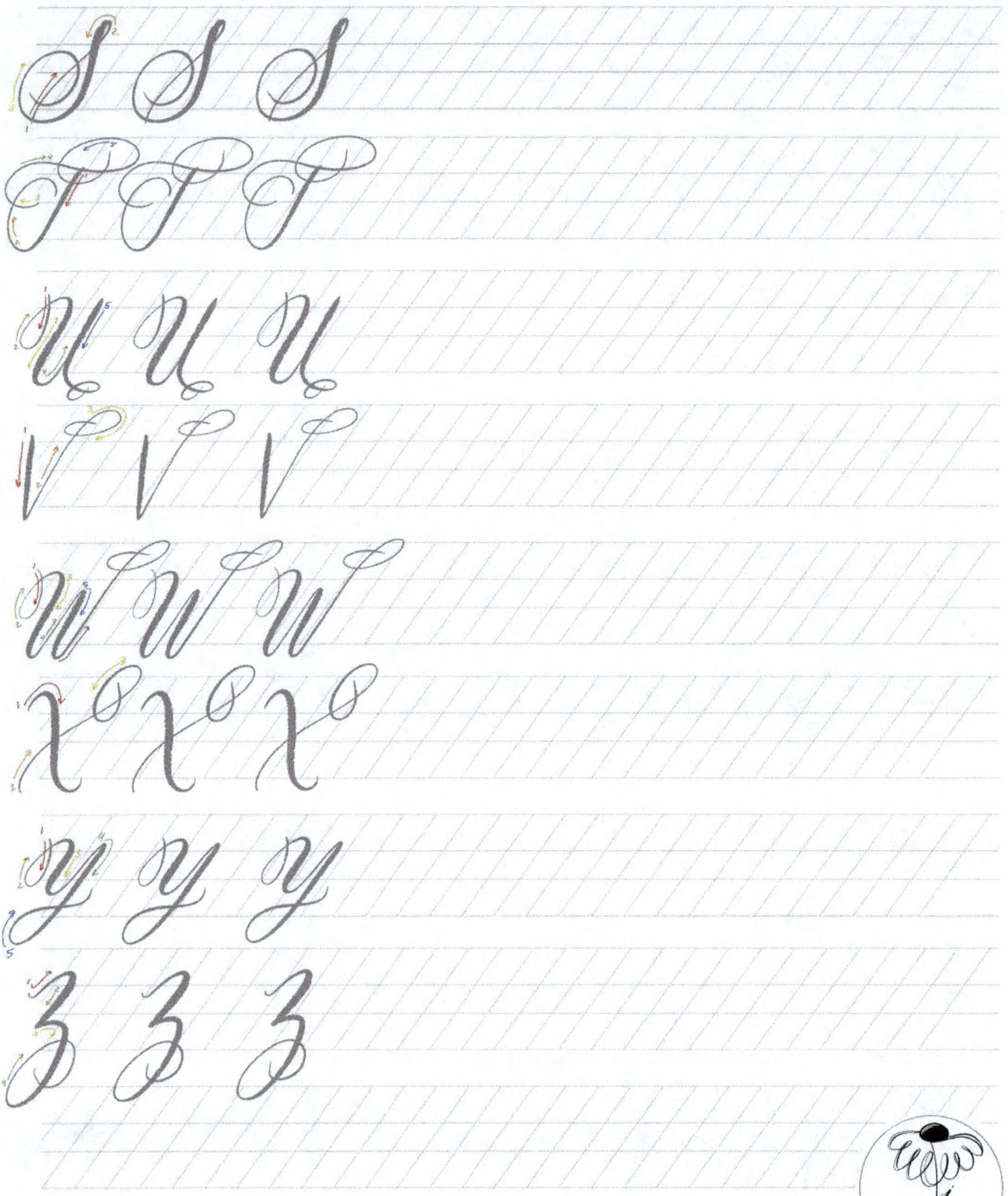

S S S

T T T

U U U

V V V

W W W

X X X

Y Y Y

Z Z Z

a a a a

b b b

c c c

d d d

e e e

f f f

g g g

h h h

i i i

One

Two

Three

Four

Five

Six

Seven

Eight

Nine

LETTER A

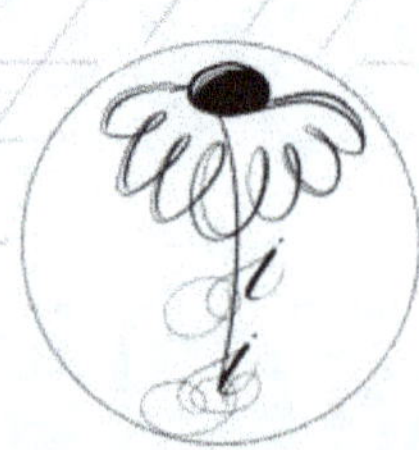

LETTER B

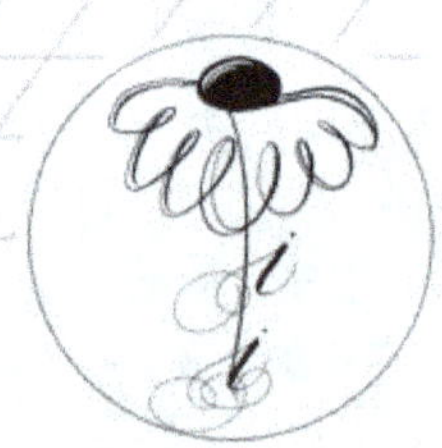

LETTER C

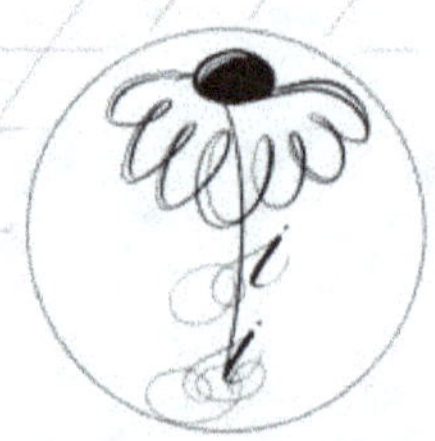

LETTER D

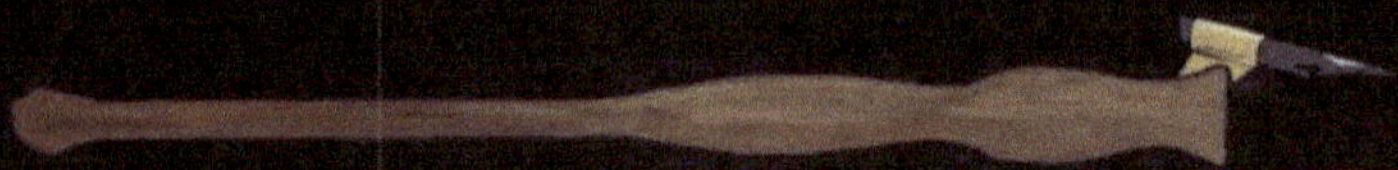

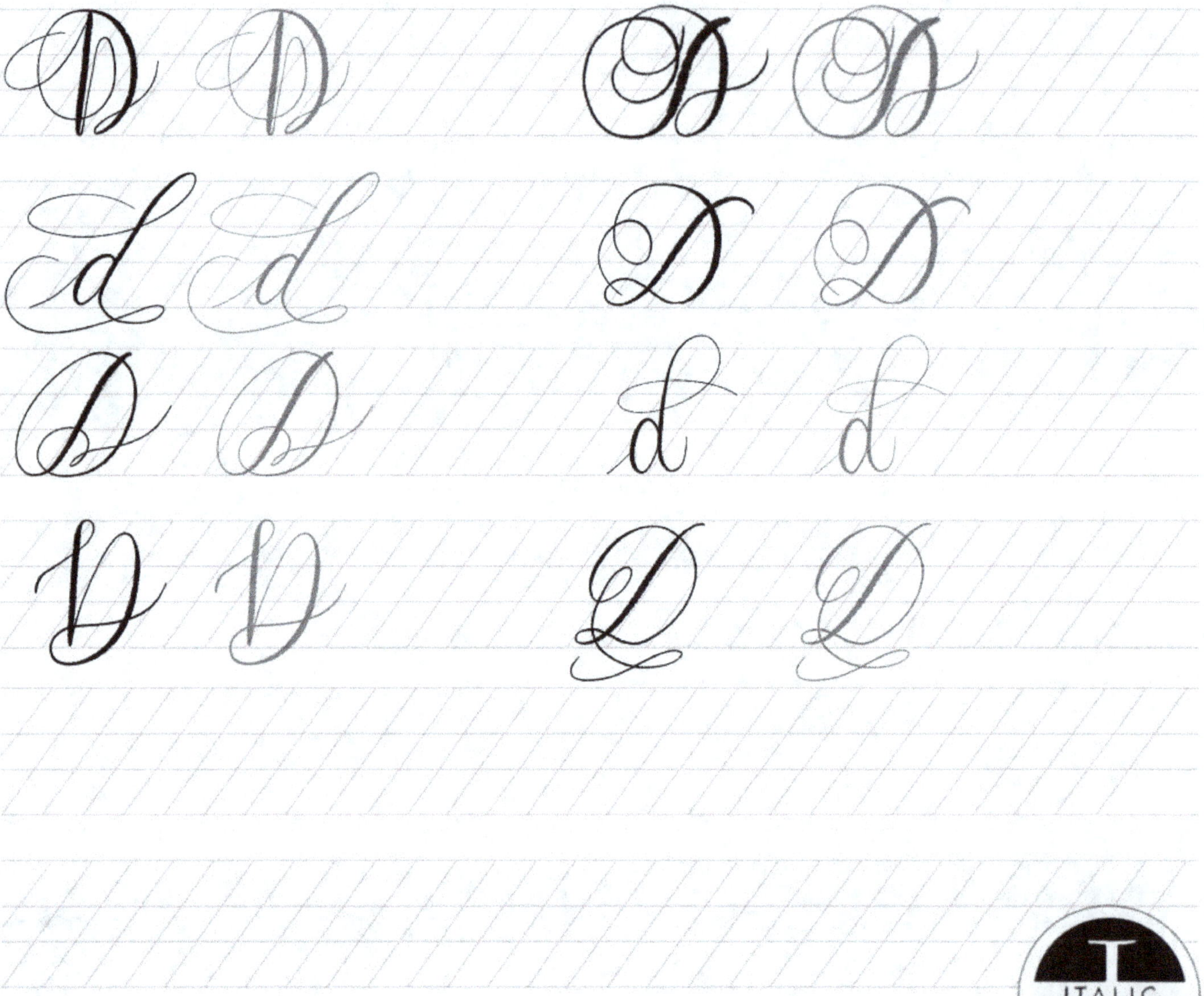

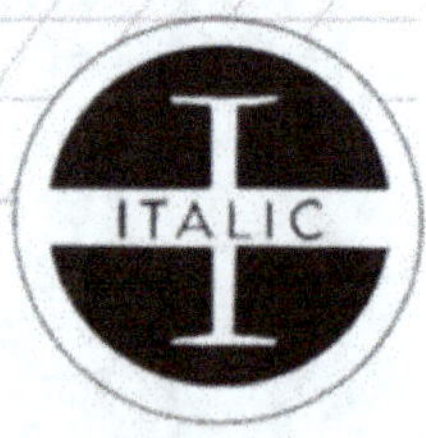

LETTER E

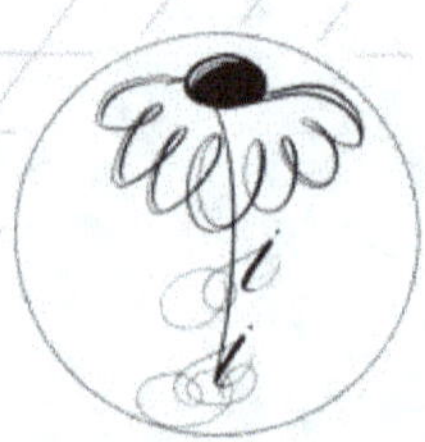

LETTER F

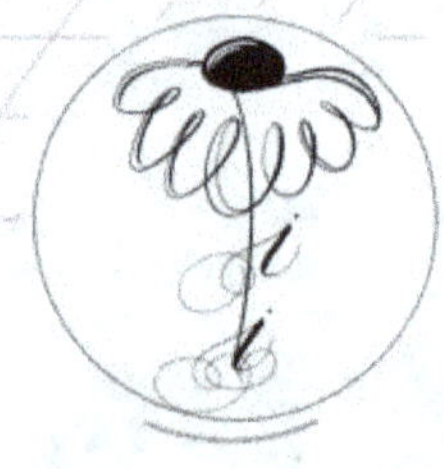

LETTER G

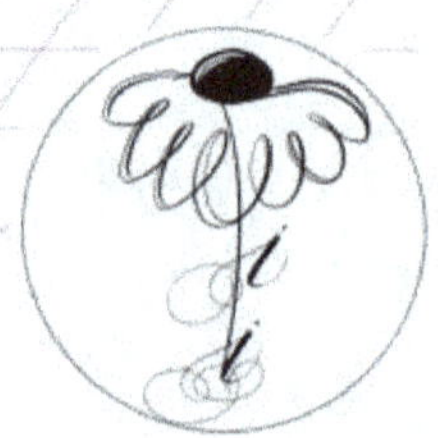

LETTER H

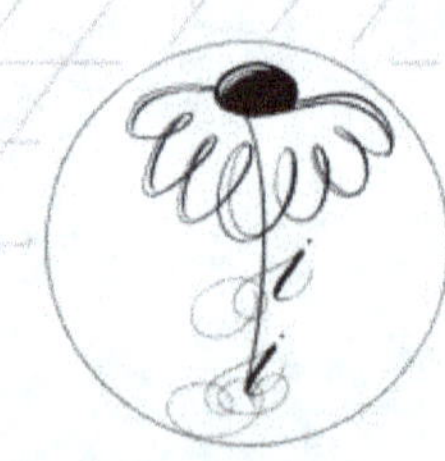

LETTER I

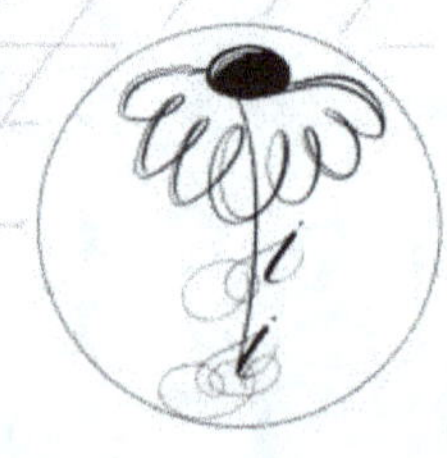

LETTER J

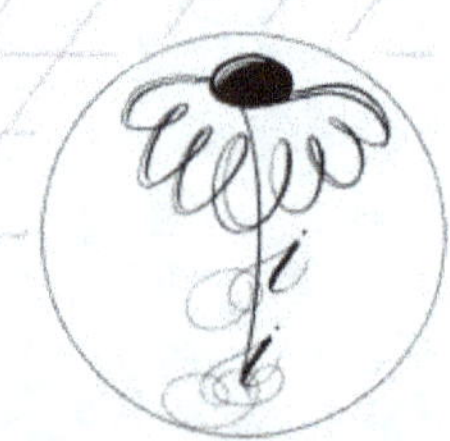

LETTER K

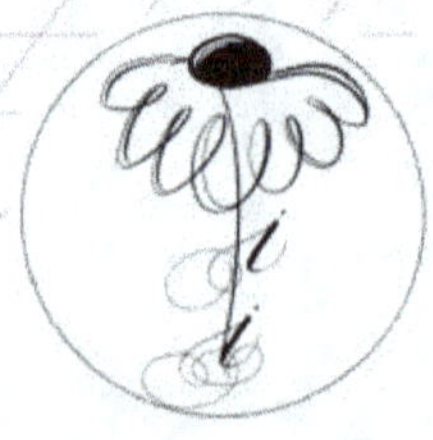

LETTER L

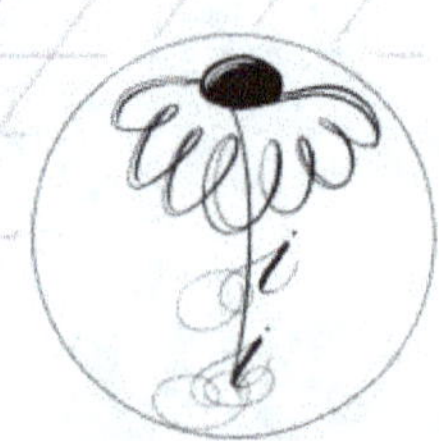

LETTER M

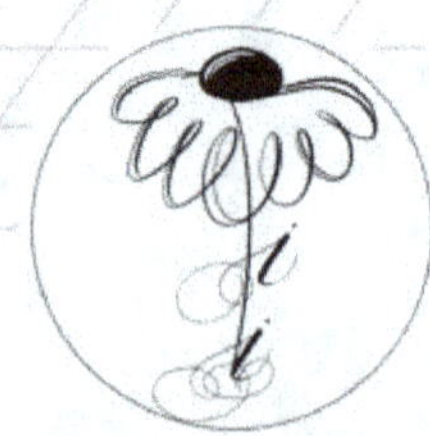

LETTER N

LETTER O

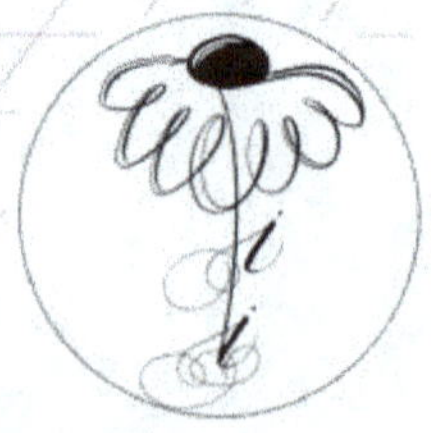

LETTER P

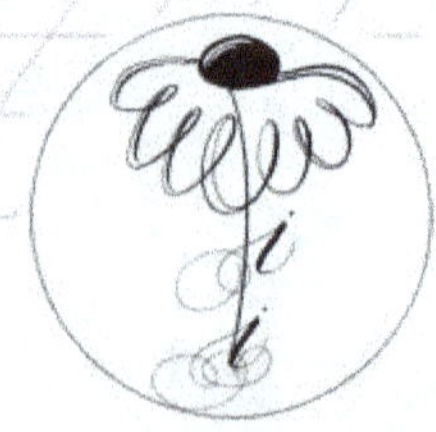

LETTER Q

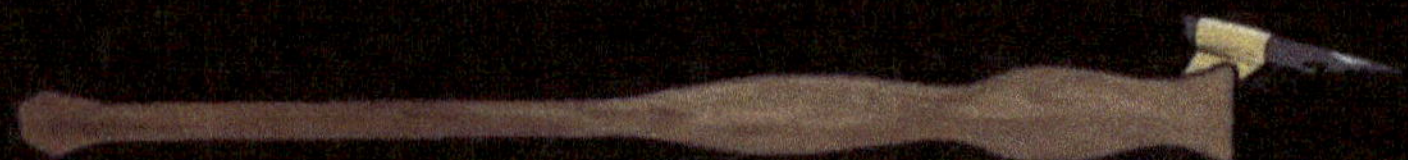

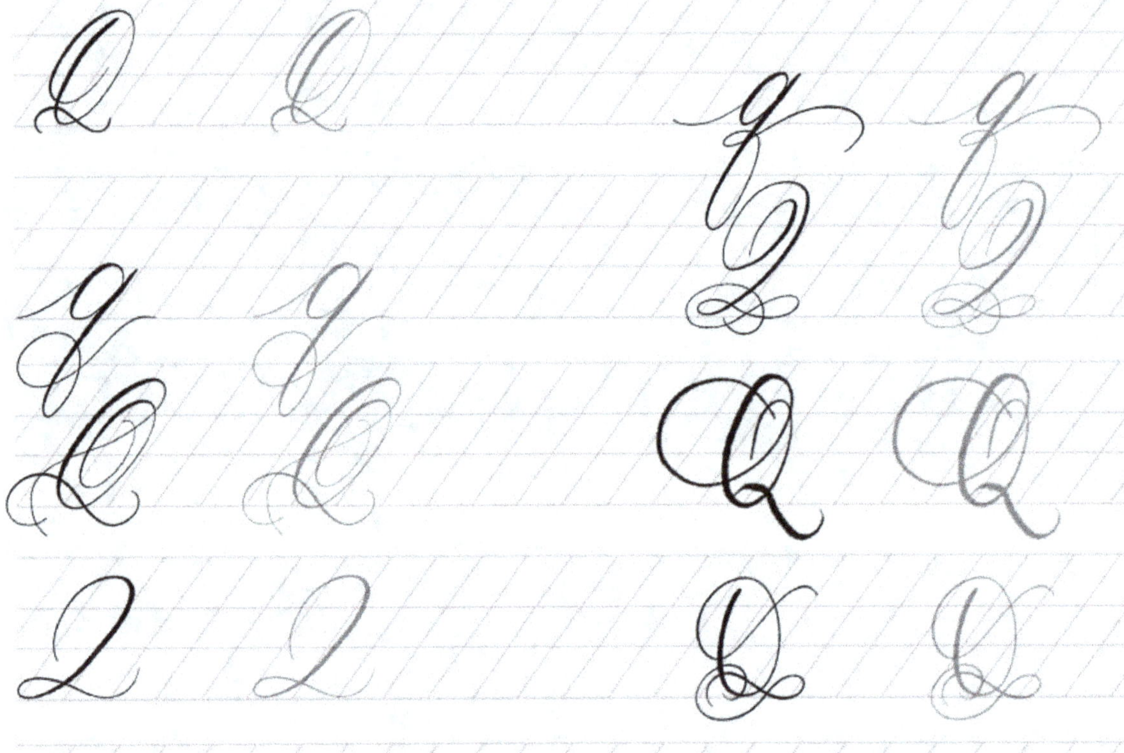

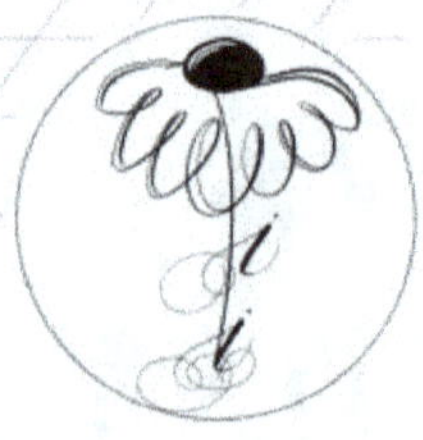

LETTER R

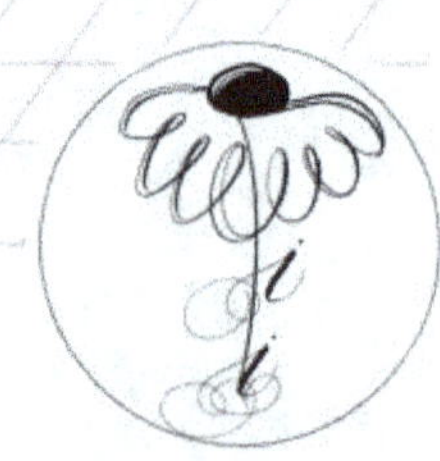

LETTER S

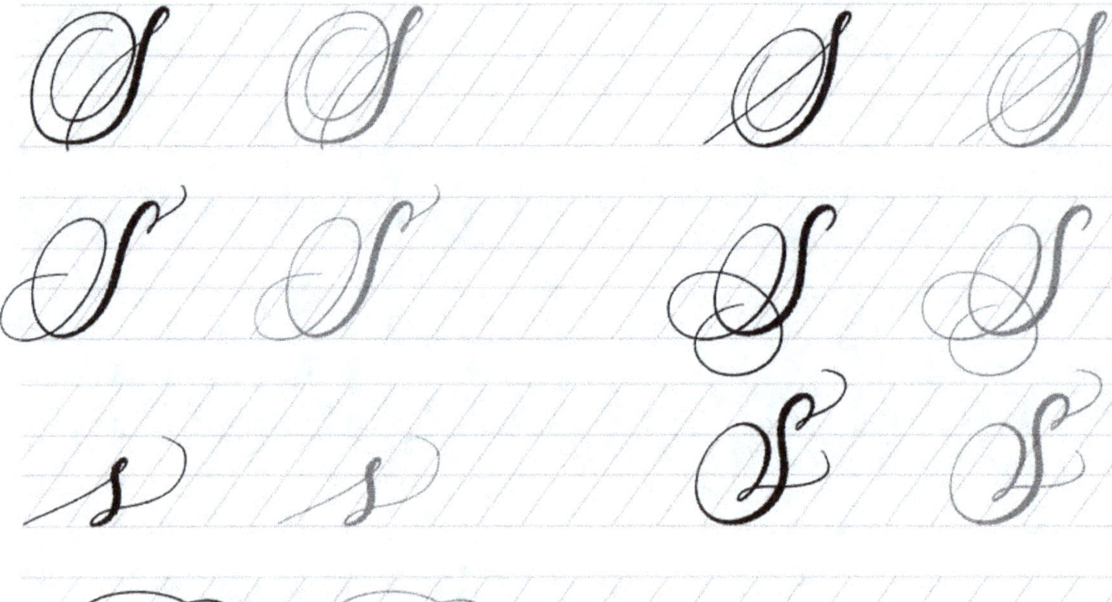

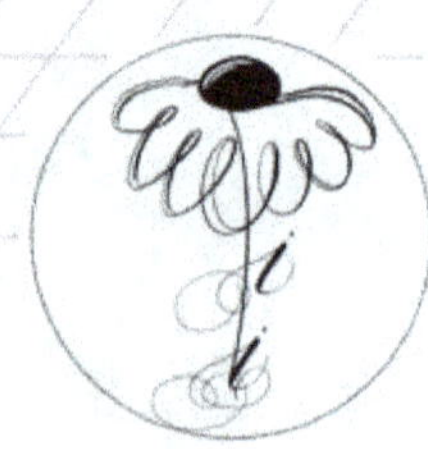

LETTER T

LETTER U

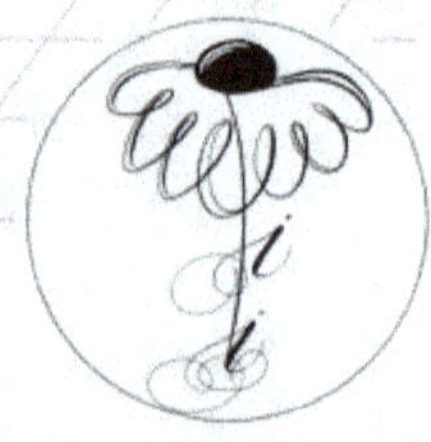

LETTER V

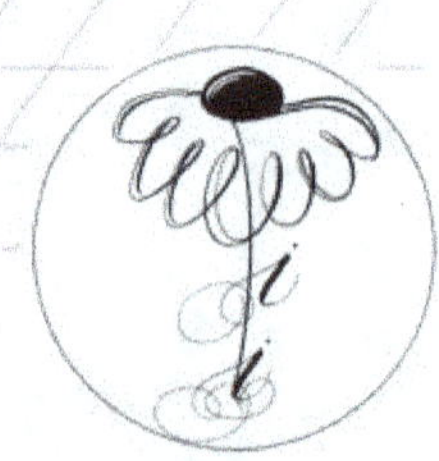

LETTER W

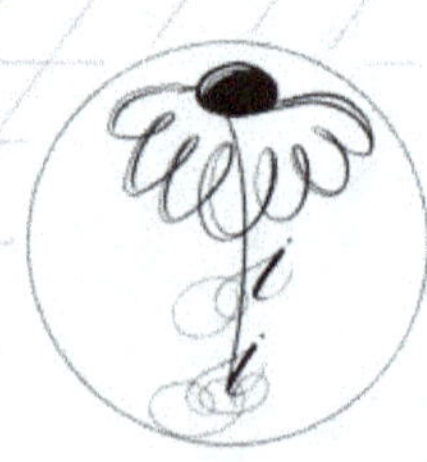

LETTER X

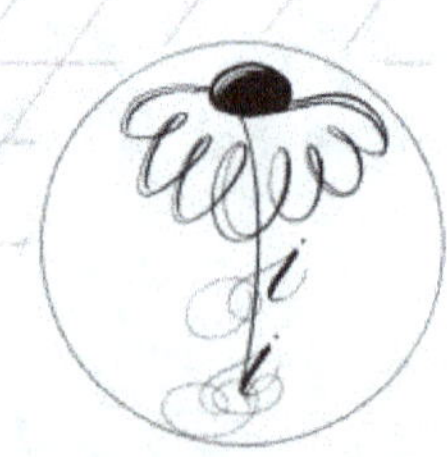

LETTER Y

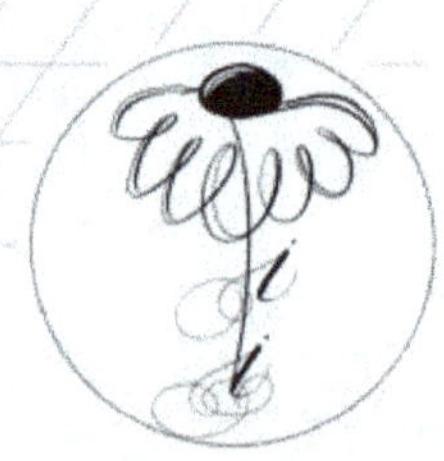

LETTER Z

See, Try, Do

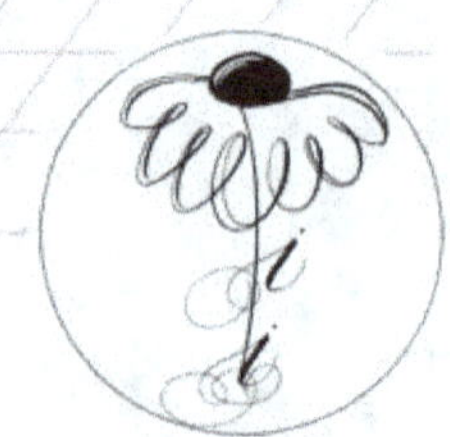